CHANGING Weather
THE STORY OF JUNE BACON–BERCEY

Written by Ashlee Klemm

Illustrated by Vanessa Toye

To my hardworking and dedicated mother.
—AK

To Cassy.
—VT

It was almost time to go live when the production manager hung up the phone and turned to his producers with a look of panic on his face.

"Benny is not going to make it. We've got to find someone else."

Frank Benny was the lead weather anchor at Buffalo, New York's, Channel 2 News. He couldn't come to work, and there wasn't much time to find a replacement before the upcoming broadcast.

WEATHER

Just several months prior to this day, the station had hired a new science reporter, but would the new journalist be willing to fill the position with such short notice? The newcomer was full of potential and determination, and even was a scientist—a meteorologist! The credentials didn't stop there; this meteorologist also studied broadcast journalism. But would station executives approve? Would viewers accept the replacement?

The decision to move forward was more complicated than it should have been. You see, it was 1971. And that incredibly knowledgeable science reporter? That reporter was a woman—an African-American woman.

Her name was June Bacon-Bercey.

June was born in 1928 in Wichita, Kansas. When June was a young girl, schools were unfairly divided, or segregated, based on skin color. African-American children were cruelly denied access to opportunities that some of their Caucasian peers seemed to take for granted. America had a lot yet to learn about equality, but this did not stop June.

She had taken an interest in the atmosphere from an early age and was encouraged to pursue meteorology by a teacher who recognized her interest in science. June's trajectory was set, and she would not accept "no" as an option.

June went on to study at the University of Kansas and later at the University of California in Los Angeles, where she was advised by a respected advisor to drop meteorology and pursue home economics instead.

It was not common for women to study science in 1950s America, and it was unheard of for an African-American woman to do so.

But June persisted on her course, and in 1954, she became the first African-American woman to earn a degree in meteorology.

June went on to work as a meteorologist at the US Atomic Energy Commission. By this time she had married and started a family. She had two daughters. It was hard working outside of the home, but when June's marriage didn't work out, she became a single mother and had no other choice.

Even though she was busy, June never stopped learning. She began to take courses in journalism on the side, and when a small position at Buffalo's news channel opened up, June was more than qualified, so she applied for the job.

She was hired.

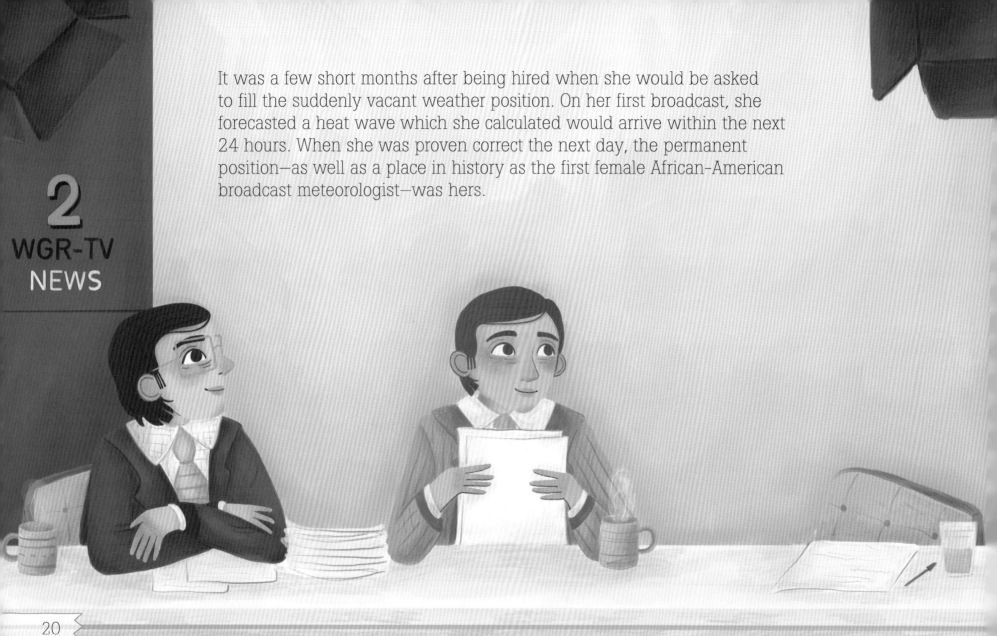

It was a few short months after being hired when she would be asked to fill the suddenly vacant weather position. On her first broadcast, she forecasted a heat wave which she calculated would arrive within the next 24 hours. When she was proven correct the next day, the permanent position—as well as a place in history as the first female African-American broadcast meteorologist—was hers.

2
WGR-TV
NEWS

She was a hit.

One year later, June Bacon-Bercey became the first African-American and the first woman to earn the American Meteorological Society's Seal of Approval.

June was a pioneer and trailblazer for women and minorities. About her accomplishments, she said, "Being a black woman, younger than my peers, everything I did I had to excel in, just to be on an even level.

"I didn't resent that," she continued. "I loved it."

Recognizing the opportunity she had to make a difference, she made up her mind to help others starting out on their own paths.

She mentored many young women and established a scholarship fund to support many others. Her lasting legacy continues to encourage and inspire today.

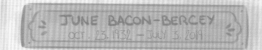

JUNE BACON-BERCEY
OCT. 23, 1932 – JULY 3, 2019